RICH OPTIONS,

POOR OPTIONS

**DATA READING IN
(F&O) IS THE HIDDEN SKILL,
ONLY RICH TRADERS USE IT**

**LEARN WHY 99% LOOSE MONEY
AND 1% MAKE MONEY IN OPTION BUYING**

INDIA'S ONE & ONLY GITA
ON DATA READING IN F&O

RICH OPTIONS,

DATA READING IN (F&O) IS THE HIDDEN SKILL, ONLY RICH TRADERS USE IT

POOR OPTIONS

LEARN WHY 99% LOOSE MONEY AND 1% MAKE MONEY IN OPTION BUYING

GUNJAN ARORA

Worldwide Published by
Pendown Press

PENDOWN PRESS

An ISO 9001 & ISO 14001 Certified Co.,

Regd. Office: 2525/193, 1st Floor, Onkar Nagar-A,

Tri Nagar, Delhi-110035

Ph.: 09350849407, 09312235086

E-mail: info@pendownpress.com

Branch Office: 1A/2A, 20, Hari Sadan, Ansari Road,

Daryaganj, New Delhi-110002

Ph.: 011-45794768

Website: PendownPress.com

First Edition: 2023

ISBN: 978-93-5554-628-9

CONTENTS

I ACKNOWLEDGE

I have gone through many phases in my 8-year stock market career. I have dealt with both positive and negative situations in the market, but even during the challenging times, I managed to approach them in a positive manner. If I hadn't gone through that phase of studying, I wouldn't have known about data reading and the value of time correction concept in the stock market.. I will discuss these aspects in detail, like an open book, in the chapter about my journey.

This book is dedicated to all my teachers, coaches, and mentors who have had an impact on my life in any way. Without them, I would never have reached this point! Now, I want to express my gratitude to those individuals who will be entering my life and bringing about the changes that every person desires but rarely finds someone to walk with them hand in hand.

I am deeply grateful to Mrs. Suman Bharti, who worked on my mindset and psychology when I was going through a challenging phase.

I would like to express my gratitude to Mr. Saurabh, who stood by my side and provided support when I needed it the most.

I want to express my deepest gratitude to my family, who have supported me in every decision I have made. Whenever I stumbled in life, my mother and father provided unwavering support. Especially my wife, who entrusted me by allowing me to sell her gold bangles, which I used as capital for trading. I also want to thank my both kids for allowing me to spare my time for learning and building my empire, I admit that I have stolen this time from their time. Their support has been invaluable to me.

AUTHOR'S NOTE

Shooting Straight from my heart, Its worth Reading

Namaskar, Aadab, Sat Sri Akal, Te Ki Haal Chaal...?

Hello everyone,

I am Gunjan Arora, Options Trader, F&O Data Reading Expert, Mentor, Author & Entrepreneur. I have more than 8 Years of experience in the industry. As of the time of writing this book, I have trained more than 12500 individuals. I have coached approximately 3200 people and mentored 400 individuals on a personal level.

I am the Creator of a Framework called **"MRSD-E", which** is being used by our academy's students and they are generating profitable returns from Options Trading in the Indian Stock Market. I am the founder of **"Trading As Profession Academy"** & I am proud to Say that we are the only one who Teaches about the **DATA READING CONCEPTs** along with Time Correction concept on chart & Super Structures of Price Action in India, While I do not wish to boast, it fills me with great pride when our academy's students, who range from beginners to highly experienced individuals with 15-20 years of experience, proclaim that our academy is the best in India. They express gratitude for how we are positively impacting the lives of retail traders in India.."

I feel a great sense of pride as I come closer and closer to achieving my goal and fulfilling my mission of helping the retail community of Indian option traders.

One more feather on the cap is that we are developing our software for in house purposes serving multiple domains like Data Reading, Trade Management Systems, Copy Trading & High Frequency Traders.

My stock market journey started back in 2012 when my uncle told me about it and he suggested that I invest in an IPO and a few stocks. I belong to a business class family and money was not a problem for me, so I invested a good amount initially and got some returns as well. After some time, one of my friends said that I got a tip from a tip provider from Indore about gold and a few stocks. He offered me to put some money in a partnership in the stock market. We have started with a capital of 5-7 lacs each and we have earned 2.5 lacs from it in the 1st month itself. I was so happy that I told my father about this and I said that from now I will be going in this business and I will not continue our family business.

We had upgraded our package from Indore's company to get more and more tips. In the 2nd month we have lost 5 lacs and that was our last month's profit and half of my capital as well. This was a very awkward moment for me as I have told my parents to leave my family business for the stock markets.

Me and my friend, we decided not to continue further and stop this stock market trading from now. But, this stock market was like a blood in the mouth of a lion which was not easy to leave. We have again started it with some new tip providers but the results were very bad and we have lost moncy again. As I was from a business background, it didn't take time for me to understand that we were doing something wrong and this is not how we can earn money from stock markets.

From here my second phase of the stock market started where I have started learning about financial markets. I have researched about the best coaches and teachers and got a few names who were SEBI REGISTERED as well. I thought that these guys are well renowned and charging a huge amount of money, they are good to go for learning. I have joined many of them and they taught me about indicators like MACD, RSI, BOLLINGER

BANDS etc and some of them taught about support and resistance or price action based trading.

Honestly speaking, I was very happy after learning and again planned that I will start this business again as I felt that I was now educated in the field. But I was wrong, I was not fully educated as indicators and price action were working with a 30-35 % accuracy of results. I again lost money which made me think that it is not my cup of tea.

Now I Have Stopped Trading After Making A Huge Losses.

I met my friend after some months, when I was traveling to Dubai. We were having dinner at his place and he asked me *aur kya chal rha hai*? I was discussing routine and by chance we had started discussing trading. He was also trading in forex markets and the US stock markets as well. I told him about my bad experience and my losses and warned him for the same.

Here started my 3rd phase of the stock market journey. He told me that he is making $1000 to $2000 per day easily while doing his other businesses. He was planning to sell all his other businesses as well to shift to a full time trading career. He suggested that I take guidance from his mentor.

Next day he insisted on me again about the same and he fixed a meeting with his mentor as well. He told me about his mentor and his empire which he has built in the last 3 years all over the world. I was amazed to know that his mentor owns a personal jet and a dozens of branded luxury cars collection. I was very excited to meet him the very next day. But the next day my friend got a call from his mentor's office that he won't be able to meet us because he doesn't want to take any new students from India. I was really shocked when I heard this and I felt very embarrassed.

By the god's grace my friend was able to convince his mentor for a meeting and then decide further. Next day we went to meet his mentor and I was again shocked when I saw a younger person than me in front of me as a mentor who has achieved so much in his life at this age. While meeting him I told him about my prior experience and losses, he again refused to take me as a student because he felt that after so many losses and so much money spent on studies in India, I will not be able to pay his fee. I was again shocked when I heard about his fees. It was $ 50000 and it was approx 35 lac INR at that time. Now, I also refused to go for this after listing the fees. We left from his place that day without any further discussion.

My friend again insisted on me to go for it and this time he offered to pay on behalf of me if I have any issue in paying. When I saw this confidence in him about his mentor and his studies, I asked him to convince his mentor to take me as his mentee. He was able to convince his mentor to take me after 2 days of wait. He was also able to convince him for partial payments and he paid some money for starting my studies till the time I was staying in dubai.

I was so excited to learn from his mentor (now my mentor) about that magic for which my friend pushed me so hard. On the day 1 at my mentor's place, while learning I felt that I made a wrong investment. He was teaching about the psychological way of trading and to find a way to trade with the natural structures where you can see the nature and emotions of a trader. Earlier I was aware about the price action and indicators so I was expecting that he will give some better indicator to trade now. He was teaching something else which I have never heard about before.

After completing my 1st day I asked my friend not to continue as I was expecting something else. He again explained to me humbly that I will be thanking him after a year from now when I will be making a lot of money from stock markets. He now gave me another guarantee that he will not ask me for money back which he lended me for admission if I did not find it valuable.

I stayed in dubai for some days and took regular classes from my mentor. Initially it was not easy to understand the concept which he was teaching but slowly slowly I got the crux and light bulb on the moment when I was able to understand the concept of this business. Stock market is a business which is purely controlled by big players who know about their customers from whom they are going to make money. Their customers were us i.e. you and me who are on the other side of the table." Big players always play with the emotions of the opponent party to make money in the stock market" my mentor said . Find a way to trade with the planning of big players.

I have learnt the concept of psychological way of trading from him and started trading in Indian markets after some time. I made good money and I was happy till the time I was trading in stocks or MCX. As I started trading in the index options, I was not getting the results which I was getting in stock trading. I asked my mentor about this and he suggested another person to learn about the data reading skill in F&O.

This time he was from the USA and he was one of the best HFT traders and Pro-Desk Option traders in the world. He was managing a very huge amount of capital for his clients and he was not into teaching. He was a very dear friend to my mentor and after my mentor's recommendation he took me as a student. He was not known or approachable to the normal person. I was amazed and thrilled to learn from him about the data reading concept in Options and Future. His knowledge was out of the world. I have learnt a very deep skill about data reading from him where I was able to see everyone naked in the hammam of the data.

What I am today is because of my 2 mentors and I will not be able to forget what they did for me. No one in India was telling or teaching about these concepts and till date no one is teaching it properly. This skill is not easy to learn as it needs a lot of effort and these days no one is ready to put in their efforts.

Everybody needs fast results but trading in the stock market is not like that. You need to keep patience and do time correction in your learning phase also. I have given a lot of time to studies and am still giving more and more time daily for studying psychology.

At Trading As Profession Academy, we have created a lot of case studies, success stories and I feel a great sense of pride as I come closer and closer to achieve my goal and fulfill my mission of helping the retail community of Indian option traders.

OUR STUDENTS SPEAKS FOR US

"Trading as a profession is very unique and standalone compared to others so called course sellers. Gunjan sir's way of teaching is unique. He taught us with real -life examples and showed you how our life is not different from trading. I love his caring nature for each and every student who is associated with him. He has an abundance of very very deep knowledge, if you follow his each and every word then you will be a successful trader in life."

~Ujjwal Kumar
Dombivli, Thane

"Trading As Profession is the best academy that provides perfect knowledge of trading with mindset and anybody who likes to make their trading career only Trading As profession Academy is recommended as per my experience. Thank you Gunjan Arora sir."

~Yumnamish Singh
Assam

Trading as a professional academy is really the last & final destination of a trading journey...

You can not find any comparison of this academy in India where you will get the real success with care of you trading journey

~Pawan Kumar
Working Professional
All these reviews are published on google as well

WHAT'S INSIDE THE BOOK?

So, guys, I am not going to write a book that will put you to sleep while reading. Instead, I am creating content that is highly applicable in the market. I have designed content that focuses on the fundamentals of future & option trading, starting from the very basics.

1. Data *Ata Kaha se Hain*? Where does the data come from?

2. *Koun Log* Data *Banaty Hai*? Who creates the data?

3. OPEN Interest *kya Hota hai*? What is Open Interest?

4. Open Interest *ko* Buyers and Sellers *ke Nazar se alag-alag kaise dekha ja sakta hai?* How can (Open Interest be analyzed from the perspective of buyers and sellers?

5. Data ko use karke trade Execution *kaise karna chahiye, Uske upar bhi mein Apko kuch Achuk Tarike Bataunga?* (How should trade execution be done using data, and I will also provide you with some effective techniques)?

6. Sabse Important Topic *Hoga ki* psychology behind the data *kya hota hai.* (The most important topic will be the psychology behind the data, and I will provide a thorough explanation of it in the book.

I want each of you to grab a Highlighter and pen. *Mein yaha* Notes *Banane ka* option *de raha hoon. Aapko jo jo* point important *Lage unko* Highlights *kijiye* and *Jaha Aapko lage ki aapke yaha se* Notes create *karne Chahiye Vaha* Notes *Banaye.* I will give you some exercise in this book. *Jo karne se aapko* execution *mein madad milengi.*

I want each of you to grab a highlighter and a pen. I am providing you with the option to take notes. Highlight the points that you find important, and create notes wherever you feel it is necessary. I will give you some exercises in this book that will help you in execution.

So, let us Begin the Journey Towards a Successful "OPTION TRADING".

Chapter 1

DATA READING IN OPTION TRADING

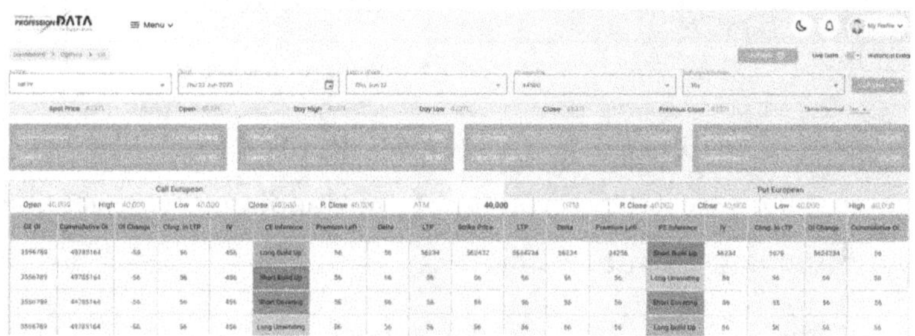

Option Trading is one of the best & highly profitable ventures, However, on the other hand, it is also highly risky due to the factor of premiums.

If you are new to the stock market, you may not be able to relate. But if you are an option trader, you can understand my words. So, let us start with the origin of Future and Option Trading.

F&O

Future and Option Trading originated in Japan. The Dojima Rice Exchange was founded back in 1697 and was the world's first organized commodities future exchange. While It may not have been highly organized, trades were able to speculate on the prices of rice through this exchange.

In the above paragraph, I mentioned the word **"speculate,"** which is the key point behind the introduction of Future & Option Trading by big businesses.

Speculation *ko Hum Hindi Mein Satta Kehta hai Ya Anuman Lagana Kehta Hai.*

(In Hindi, **"speculation"** can be translated as "gambling" or "making an estimate.")

Now, try to grasp the main need of the future and option segment. This will help you in understanding the psychology behind the data in future chapters.

When a Businessman (I would like to refer to him using two more words- trader and speculator in any writing to attach your emotions in understanding) wants to speculate on the price of a particular asset, stock, commodity, or currency, he assumes that the price will move in his desired direction. He also takes measures to ensure the same.

CRUX is Hidden Here!
"BIG PLAYERS Always Assume,
Plan And Than EXECUTE!

Big players have the capacity to make the right decisions. However, as a retail trader, I always believed that when a particular company seals a deal, its stock prices either show an immediate increase on the same day or move up the following day.

~But this is not the Truth.

The truth is, if you are receiving news on television, social media, or any other medium, you are the last person receiving it.

Now, ask yourself, "Were you someone who used to think like this previously?"

Now, the second reason for the existence of the F&O market was short selling. Many of you may be aware of short selling, but I want to provide you with a new perspective on it.

"Short Selling" is used in the stock market to make profit from a decrease in the price of stocks or assets. In short selling, traders borrow shares from brokers and sell them in the market, aiming to buy them back at a lower price in the future. It's a high-risk strategy because the potential loss is unlimited.

In India, we cannot use short selling positionally. We can only sell a stock for intraday if we don't have it in our demat account.

In the F&O segment, one can sell positionally in two ways. Firstly, they can sell a future, and second, they can buy a put option to express their bearish intention. By selling a future of a particular asset, they can buy a future of a particular position until the expiry. I will explain expiry as well in upcoming chapters. By buying a "Put Option", they have a limited liability as they paid the premium.

Now, what is Premium? I will cover the concept of premium as well in the upcoming chapter. Honestly, understanding premium is one of the most important concepts that should be learned by "Option Traders".

Now, coming to the main part of the story, all these transactions are recorded by a government entity. In India, the NSE (National Stock Exchange) is responsible for recording and managing all types of Future and Option transactions.

These transactions are recorded in a contract format, and each formed contract creates an "Open Interest."

"Open Interest" is formed when a contract is first created, and it is calculated as the "Open Interest" until it remains active or expires.

In the next chapter, we will discuss open interest in detail.

"Understanding Open Interest Is The Key
To Be A Profitable Option Trader."

~Gunjan Arora

Chapter 2

HOW DOES OPEN INTEREST FORM?

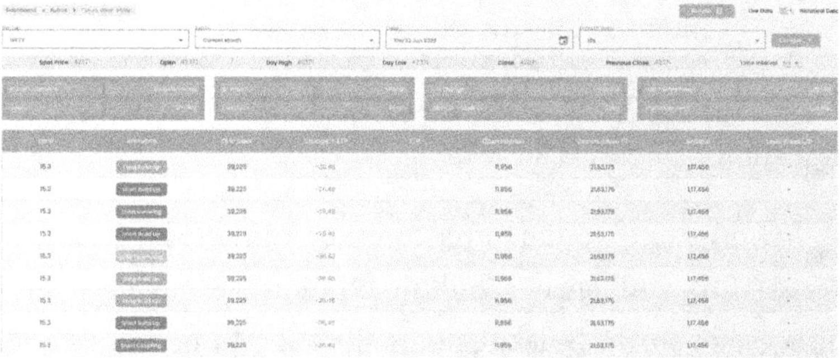

In Futures & Option Trading, it is not possible to trade without knowledge of open interest. When I am talking about Open Interest here, I want you to pay full attention to reading this part and this chapter. I am going to provide you with a few exercises as well that you should do to gain a better understanding of Option Trading.

The creation of a new contract results in the formation of Open Interest. Here, creation means when a contract is initiated for the first time by any party. I will provide more details on the parties involved in the next chapter to enhance your understanding.

To delve deeper into understanding open interest (OI), you should also be familiar with a few more terms. There are two types of communities in F&O trading.

1st- Buyer Community

2nd- Seller Community

- The Buyers' Community can create open interest (OI) by buying future or call/put Options.

- Similarly, the Seller Community can create open interest (OI) by selling future or call/put Options.

These two lines may seem simple to read, but they form the foundation of F&O data reading.

When we refer to the buyer community, they can create open interest (OI) and open a bullish position by buying a future contract of a stock, Index, Commodity, etc. In option, they can create both bullish & bearish positions.

Yes, here is the CRUX!

The buyers' community can create both bullish and bearish directional trades by buying a call option and buying a put option, respectively.

On the other hand, the sellers community can create open interest (OI) by entering into a bearish directional trade by selling a future contract of any tradable asset.

They can also trade in options and can create open interest (OI) with both bullish and bearish positions. They can sell call options to enter a bearish trade and sell put options to enter a bullish directional trade.

Now, In the above two paragraphs, I have mentioned 3+3=6 types of contract creations where open interest (OI) is formed.

I want you to write down all six situations where contract creations are happening. It will give You clarity.

Here's a tip: Highlight the important lines in above paragraph.

Chapter 3

WHY IS THE OPTION CHAIN IS INCOMPLETE?

Option Chain is the Cover of the Book

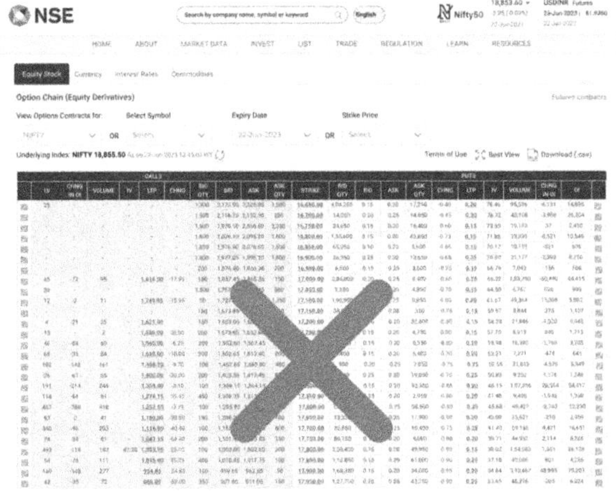

When discussing the data of option and future, one often envisions an option chain. This perception has been influenced by social media, where influencers have portrayed the option chain as a superhero.

One of my mentors from the USA once shared a quote about the option chain with me, stating, "Option chain is the cover page of the book; you cannot judge a book by its cover." When

I inquired further, he explained that the option chain displays the total number of transactions or open contracts for a specific asset. However, this is not the proper way to study or analyze the data.

Data should be analyzed by delving deeper into specific strike prices and observing different time frames during live market sessions. Moreover, data should be studied by combining multiple strike prices with each other.

All of this should be done within the framework of a particular strategy, which incorporates data from option buyers, option sellers, and future traders.

When I mention multiple strike prices here, I mean that you need to check data for at-the-money (ATM), slightly in-the-money (ITM), and slightly out-of-the-money (OTM) strike prices. This is because when a big player enters or exits a position, they typically trade in multiple strikes.

"You Can Feel The Emotion of A Trader By Analyzing Data."

~Gunjan Arora

If you can deeply understand the data, believe me, you will be able to sense the emotions of a trader. However, achieving this requires a significant amount of practice and dedication towards learning the skill.

In the next chapter, I will guide you through a thorough study. I encourage all of you to join me in delving deep into the studies.

Chapter 4

DATA OF OPTION BUYERS

This will be the key factor for execution, if you are an a option buyer

As mentioned earlier, I am writing this book to provide you with real help, and that will be your execution point.

I always tell my students in the academy that strategy alone does not work. Only traders who can use a strategy with correct emotions and timing can achieve results.

That's why it is important to be a strategy maker, not just a strategy user. I am referring here to strategy creation and using it according to the current market situation.

> *"Every Day, Stock Market Requires Different Types of Attention."*

How is it possible to use the same strategy in every market situation? Have you ever heard of someone driving a car at the same speed every single minute or encountering the same traffic on the road? There can be heavy traffic, causing one to slow down, and there can be an empty road where one can speed up. Think about why I shared the above story. I want you to pay attention to one thing: that you have to adapt and perform in different ways in the market daily.

"People Have Different Emotions Daily, So Does The Market."

You need to be a strategy maker so that you can make decisions based on the market situation.

I know that when it comes to option trading, many myths exist in people's minds. This is because there is a lot of noise on social media these days. Everyday, you come across a new strategy on YouTube and try to implement it in the live market with real money. When it doesn't work, you continue for a day or two, and then you find another one on YouTube again.

Just Remember My Words:

"Strategy Does Not Work; A Trader With The Right Execution And Mindset Can Create Magic With Any Strategy."

~Gunjan Arora

You may often worry about whether to do option buying or option selling. Many social media influencers create content about "Theta is the enemy for option buyers; only option sellers can make money; option buyers can't make money."

Now, pay attention. I promise you that if you understand the concept of "Data Reading" in F&O, you can make money in both option buying and option selling.

Option buying needs special care and attention while trading in the live market. You can read the data of option buyers separately

In the previous chapter, you learned about open interest and the buyer and seller communities.

When an option buyer wants to trade in a particular direction, they create open interest by buying an option.

We will now learn about this in great detail. Let's take an example of bullish direction here. If an option buyer wants to trade in a bullish direction, they can buy a call option.

When they buy a call option, a separate open interest is created, and its data is segregated on the NSE server. This open interest (OI) can be read separately. Now, the question arises: where can this data be seen? Don't worry, I will guide you on this in the upcoming chapter.

- An important point to learn here is that you can access the data of an option buyer.

The open interest by option buyers can be understood by a term used in data reading is called "Long Buildup" This long build up can only be done by the buyer community.

When these contracts made by option buyers are squared off, it is called "Long Unwind".

Long unwind can only be performed by option buyers. At this time, the open interest calculation will be subtracted from the total OI of an option buyer.

One more point to remember here is that when option buyers square off their option, as mentioned above, the open interest will be subtracted or decreased. You will understand this point in the next chapter.

So let's move forward with the data of option sellers. I want you guys to highlight important points from the above content and make handwritten notes.

In the area below, write down the understanding you gained from "Option Buyers Data".

Chapter 5

DATA OF OPTION SELLER'S

Must Know About their Activities: Theta, Delta, Vega, I.V

As we have discussed in previous chapters, data can be checked separately for option buyers and sellers.

You need to understand the psychology behind the data of option sellers. when I say the psychology behind the data, I mean their plans, mindset, emotions. When they are in fear, when they are looking for more profits, this can be checked in the F&O data.

I have learned from many people in India, and I have not seen traders talking about the psychology of other traders to make their trading decisions. If you are able to identify the above sentiments of other human traders in charts and data, believe me, you can make a hell lot of money.

The community discussed in the last chapter was the option buyer community. Usually, big players trade as a seller community, except when they are very sure about making more profits. Option sellers are cash-rich communities because margin requirements for selling options are very high due to the high risk involved.

Now, the most important point to learn here is that the person with a huge amount of money has the capacity to move a particular asset or market as per their desire, and option selling is the segment that requires a significant amount of margin. So not everyone can trade in this segment. As of now, when i am writing this book, 1 lot of index options requires around 1.5 lakh INR as margin.

Big players have the advantage that they don't face huge competition in this segment. They also have some more benefits in selling options. One of these benefits is Theta Decay. Theta is the time value, and it is one of the Greeks involved in calculation of options premium. I am not going to teach you about Greeks here as this is theoretical knowledge. I will be teaching you about the practical use of a few Greeks.

Theta Decay/Vega/Delta, these three Greeks are very important to understand, and that too practically.

THETA

Theta denotes the time value involved in the premium (price) of an option. These Greeks are calculated by the Black Scholes method, which is a mathematical model for the dynamics of a derivative instrument. It is used to price option contracts, which require five input variables.

1. The strike price of an option.

2. The current stock price.

3. The time to expire.

4. The risk-free rate.

5. The validity.

Don't worry, you don't need to calculate all these manually. I will let you know in the upcoming chapter about software where you can check this activity for free.

Now, back to the topic of option selling, theta value is the time value or interest amount in easy language that has to be paid to the lender at the end of the day, whether you have earned money or not. Time value has to be decreased on a daily basis.

Many of you may have heard from social media influencers that theta is the enemy of an option buyer - this is wrong.

I don't buy this thought about theta. Theta is a value that has to be deducted in 24 hours, and it is almost fixed. So for intraday players, it will not affect much, and if you want to hold your position in options, it is the pre-planned risk that should be taken care of while entering into a trade.

Theta value is a benefit for a non-directional option seller. As an option seller, you have the liberty to hold the position as a particular amount in the form of Theta will definitely be your profit.

Delta

Delta Value is the value that estimates the change in the price of an option contract compared to its underlying asset. For example, if the Delta of a particular strike price is (+70), that means theoretically that option will move Rs. 70 compared to the index movement of Rs. 100.

VEGA

Vega is the most important point to understand. Vega is the risk metric that measures an option's price sensitivity to change. It is the most important factor for an option because it is a dynamic value that changes with the demand of that option contract.

Implied volatility & Vega are like brother and sister. These values can make a lot of difference in your trading career. I will be teaching you about Implied volatility in the upcoming chapter.

The above knowledge of the Greeks involved was necessary to give you a strong foundation

Now, coming to the open interest part, when the seller community sells an option contract, a separate open interest (OI) gets created, and it can be scanned in data separately.

Similarly to option buying, when a seller sells a contract, open interest forms, and the data gets segregated on NSE servers, which can be seen in their paid version. I will also suggest a software for you.

The open interest (OI) created here can be identified in the data by a term called "short build-up." "Short build-up" means sellers can create fresh positions, and this can only be done by the seller community.

When these contracts are squared off, meaning the seller community books their profit or loss, it can be seen as "short covering" in option data. During short covering, the option interest will decrease instead of increasing.

We will be discussing short build-up and short covering in a separate chapter as it is a very important point to understand.

Now, moving forward to the data of futures, which also plays an important role in making trading decisions. I want each one of you to highlight important points and write them down below:

____

____

____

____

____

____

____

Chapter 6

DATA OF FUTURES CONTRACT

Till now, we have discussed the data of option buyer & option seller. Now, we are going to discuss the data of futures.

It is equally important to the option data. Big players trade in both future and option selling. They trade in option buying only when they want to scalp and have a clear plan.

Futures data for index & stock futures, which are tradable, can be checked on NSE paid data services separately. When a trader executes an order in a future contract, whether buying or selling, a separate open interest (OI) is formed. When future contract traders want to enter into a bullish trade, they can buy a future contract of that particular stock, index, or any tradable asset. This creates a separate OI, which is shown as "long buildup" in the data.

On the other hand, when a trader wants to enter into a bearish trade, they can sell a future contract of that particular asset. This also creates a separate (OI), form which is shown as "short buildup" in the data.

Similarly, at the time of booking profit or loss, traders will square off their positions. This data will be shown as "long unwinding" in the case of buyers and "short covering" in the case of sellers.

I will be teaching you in detail about the calculation of open interest (OI) in a separate chapter.

These three types of data that we have learned so far are key factors to be checked for execution.

In the next chapter, we will discuss the effects of implied volatility, global market effects, and how to execute a trade using all these data factors.

Before moving forward, I want you all to highlight important points and make notes of your understanding.

Chapter 7

CALCULATION OF OPEN INTEREST

Terminology Used in Data

This is the most important aspect in option trading because we are playing with numbers, and numbers should be treated very carefully. In any business, numbers can change the game, and you should keep in mind that numbers in option and future can only be seen in open interest.

Now, many of you follow option chain as we are motivated by YouTube or all the social media educational environment, and everyone is creating content on option chain. My mentor once said to me, "Gunjan, Option Chain Is Only The Cover Of A

Book, And We Cannot Judge The Content Properly By Looking At Its Cover."

When I first learned about the concept of Data Reading in depth, I was like, *"kya ye sach me hota hai?"* In India, most traders or coaches use price action, candlestick patterns, and chat patterns to make trading decisions. But this was something else that I was experiencing. Frankly speaking, I wasn't able to trust my mentor at first. I thought that data may work in the USA, but after learning it properly, I realized that this is the most important concept for trading in the future & option segment.

My learning experience about the data was not so pleasant as I was learning from a mentor who is from the USA and focused on F&O data. All the numbers were really difficult to understand as they looked the same. However, my mentor supported me during that time and guided me throughout my journey. He once said to me, "When I was losing hopes,, You have to work hard to learn about this data. Success takes an investment in time, dedication, and sacrifice. This is true education; it's a process."

Now, you may wonder why I have shared my hard story of learning with you. I have shared it because I want to shorten your learning curve. It took me several years to learn how to decode the data for Indian markets. I went through several failures before achieving success. It was because I didn't have access to Indian market data.

So, I want to encourage you that during this learning process, you may feel like giving up or face failures that block your way. But don't give up.

Now, coming to the topic of the calculation of open interest. The first thing to keep in mind is that we have to combine and calculate all the numbers of option buyers, sellers and futures to make an execution decision. We have the liberty to analyze the data of option buyers, sellers & futures separately. Let's understand each one in detail.

Option Buyer's & Future buyer's belong to the buyers community. The buyers community can only create open interest (OI) by buying a contract, and this is Known as "long buildup."

Long buildup represent the position of buyers community and there is a calculation involved in this process.

When a trader from the buyers community, whether it's a call buyer, put buyer, or a future contract buyer, executes a trade, a new fresh open interest is created.

| | PUTS | | | |
STRIKE	VOLUME	NET CHNG	LTP	OI
42100	0	0	151.75	1,32,200
42100	58,700	7.4	159.15	1,32,200
42100	7,16,975	20.55	172.3	2,26,675
42100	13,50,500	21.25	173	2,68,750
42100	19,77,825	56.4	208.15	3,26,050
42100	25,99,875	-7.45	144.3	3,91,100
42100	30,69,675	23.15	174.9	4,12,800
42100	34,23,825	10.15	161.9	4,35,400
42100	43,12,000	48.2	199.95	4,69,925
42100	49,38,575	64.9	216.65	4,49,150
42100	54,12,400	68.8	220.55	4,52,600
42100	60,03,075	78.25	230	4,60,175
42100	65,02,400	93.5	245.25	4,89,150
42100	74,33,975	78.5	230.25	5,17,825
42100	76,64,900	76.45	228.2	5,69,550

If we observe a regular increase in the open interest in the data, it means that new fresh contracts are being added more and more. However, one important point to note is that in the case of the buyer community, the price of that particular option or future will also increase along with the open interest (OI).

Now, let's understand what happens when "buyers community" traders book their profit or loss. When an option buyer, whether it's a call buyer, put buyer, or a future contract buyer, squares off his position, the open interest reduces, and the price also decreases accordingly. This situation is referred to as "long unwinding," and it can only be done only by the buyer's community.

Now, let's discuss the seller community. When a trader from the "seller's community" wants to sell a call option (bearish position) or a put option (bullish position) or a seller of a future contract (bearish position) executes a trade, a new and fresh open interest (OI) is created. This is referred to as "short buildup."

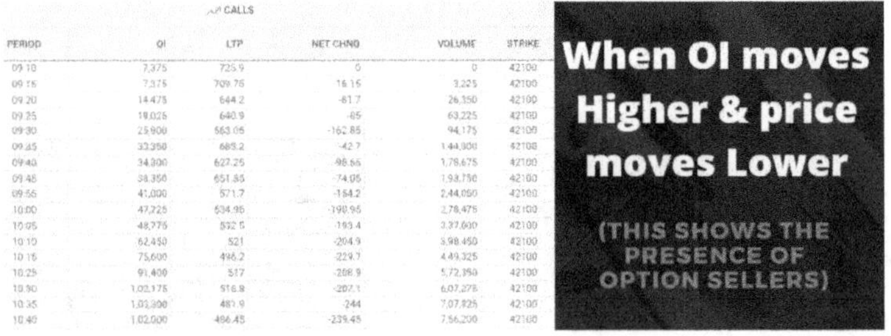

	CALLS				
PERIOD	OI	LTP	NET CHNG	VOLUME	STRIKE
09:10	7,375	725.9	0	0	42100
09:15	7,375	709.75	-16.15	3,225	42100
09:20	14,475	644.2	-81.7	26,350	42100
09:25	19,025	640.9	-85	63,225	42100
09:30	25,900	563.05	-162.85	94,175	42100
09:35	33,350	683.2	-42.7	1,44,000	42100
09:40	34,300	627.25	-98.55	1,78,675	42100
09:45	38,350	651.85	-74.05	1,93,750	42100
09:55	41,000	571.7	-154.2	2,44,050	42100
10:00	47,225	534.95	-190.95	2,78,475	42100
10:05	48,775	532.5	-193.4	3,37,600	42100
10:10	62,450	521	-204.9	3,98,450	42100
10:15	75,600	496.2	-229.7	4,49,325	42100
10:25	91,400	517	-208.9	5,72,350	42100
10:30	1,02,175	516.8	-207.1	6,07,275	42100
10:35	1,03,300	483.9	-244	7,07,825	42100
10:40	1,02,000	486.45	-239.45	7,56,200	42100

Short buildup indicates the position of the seller's community, and we need to calculate this data accordingly.

When there is a regular increase in open interest, it means new positions are being created. However, if we observe an increase in open interest (OI) along with a decrease in the price of that particular option or future, it is called short buildup, indicating the presence of option sellers.

When the seller community wants to book their profits or losses, they will square off their running positions. This will result in a decrease in open interest (OI) and an increase in price. This process is known as "short covering."

Now, the most important aspect of understanding OI is that it allows you to perceive the emotions of traders and the overall market sentiment of these calculations.

The party that has created open interest with greater intensity will have an advantage. The more intense the numbers, the more powerful the trader on that side is perceived to be.

On the Other hand, the party that shows weakness and exits their positions at a loss, booking profits early, indicates a lack of interest in holding their positions further. This creates pressure on that particular community.

By delving deep into the calculations of open interest, we can observe emotions such as confidence, fear, and greed.

The realm of open interest is so intense that one could write a separate book solely dedicated to it. In this chapter, I have provided an overall but intense understanding of open interest. Before proceeding to the next piece of content,

I encourage each one of you to highlight the important points from this chapter and write them down based on your understanding.

____

____

____

____

____

____

____

Chapter 8

MOST IMPACT FACTOR IN OPTION TRADING

Implied Volatility

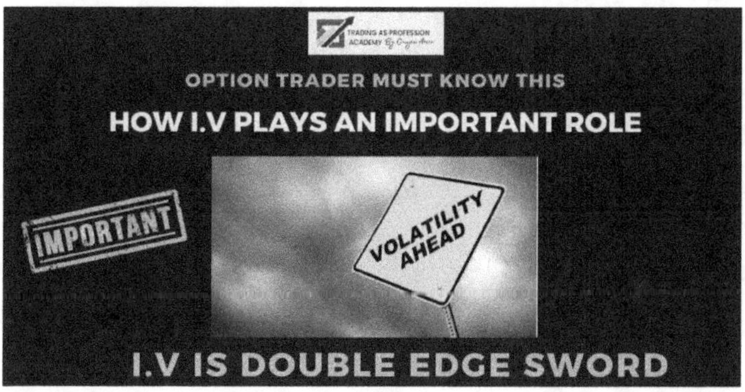

As an option trader, we often hear about Theta Decay being referred to as our enemy. The majority of teachers in India, with a few exceptions, echo this sentiment and teach the same concept. Theta only affects you when you are a positional player. This is because you already know the approximate value of the Theta that will decrease from your option in a day. If you hold an option for BTST (Buy Today Sell Tomorrow)or positionally, it signifies two things. First, you are aware of the time decay factor (Theta Decay) associated with that option, and you have a plan for it. Second, you are unaware of this factor and are holding a time bomb after removing the pin. If you don't pay attention to it, it will inevitably explode. The main drawback is that this bomb (option buying) is kept in your pocket, which means it will explode in your pocket.

"You Have To Think That In Which Situation You Are!"

Now, the most underrated aspect in the market that significantly affects the intraday option prices is IV (Implied Volatility) is closely related to Vega, which is one of the Greek formulas that make up an option. Vega indicates the impact of the volatility on the premium of an option. In this case, IV stands for implied volatility, specifically referring here to the daily live IV values that can affect option premiums.

One can make trading decisions for intraday by using implied volatility. Let's delve deeper into this content. Implied volatility can be monitored live during intraday trading hours for both CALL and PUT options separately.

It usually starts in the range of 9-10 and can go to any number. This increase is due to the uncertain risk factor associated with the option for an option seller. An Option seller is not interested to sell an option when their is uncertainty or high volatility in the market, resulting in increased demand for that particular option from option buyers community at higher prices.

I suggest you guys read the previous paragraph again and highlight it because IV plays a crucial role in option trading and can be somewhat challenging to understand.

Why is it Difficult?

I asked the same question to my mentor, and he explained that IV is like a double-edged sword (*Do Dhari Talwar*) that needs to be handled with great care. As I delved deeper into the topic, I discovered the untapped or invisible factor that my mentor was trying to convey. To be very honest, when I was learning about data from my mentor, I had moments where I felt like - *kuch samaj aa bhi raha hai and kuch nhi bhi aa raha hai!* (I understood everything and moments where I felt completely lost). That was because he was introducing concepts and ideas that I had never heard of before. I recommend reading this chapter twice or even thrice to gain a better understanding.

Now, let me teach you some important points about IV that will help you make better execution decisions.

An increase in IV on either side the CALL or PUT side indicates that the "buyer's community" is entering that side. For example, if IV increases on the CALL side, it means that option buyers are entering the CALL side.

On the other hand, a decrease in IV on either side signifies exit of an option buyer. For instance, if IV on PUT side decreases, it means that PUT buyers are closing their positions.

However, it's crucial to note that many times IV is manipulated by option sellers to increase premiums and create fake breakouts. Retail traders often trust these breakouts because they seek proof for every decision. Big players exploit this concept of proof to trap retail traders and make substantial profits.

The concept of IV is so deep that I can write a separate book on implied volatility. IV plays an important role in option trading and an option trader should be aware of all its facts. The most important part I have learnt in this was, It can be manipulated by the options sellers to increase premiums of an option, which results in fakeouts. IV should be handled very carefully.

During my learning journey with both of my mentors, they emphasized the use of psychological proof. They discouraged relying solely on chart patterns or candlestick patterns, as these are used as traps by bigger players.

In the next lesson, I will teach you about the psychology behind the data. Honestly, while writing this book, I contemplated whether to reveal this content in the book or not. But I decided to write with an open heart and the energy of a giver.

"So Fasten Your Seatbelts, The Next
Chapter Can Give You A Jhatka."

Chapter 9

PSYCHOLOGY BEHIND THE DATA

Guys if you have reached this point of the book, I'm confident that you are now on cloud nine. The content I am delivering to you is incredibly powerful, and by reading this book alone, you can grasp the core and hidden aspects of Option Trading.

In this chapter, you will discover the biggest hidden secret of Option Trading. If you concentrate fully and understand this chapter, you will realize why your stop-loss hits in intraday trading.

Option Trading has gained immense popularity worldwide, and in India, we have only weekly and monthly options expiry, whereas in the USA, they have daily, weekly, and monthly expiry. Option trading can be a money making machine, but at the same time, it can also destroy your capital. It can only generate profits for those who are educated about the options very deeply, while others risk losing their entire capital.

In India, the maximum number of retail traders are option buyers. These traders typically have a small amount of capital to begin with and have heard about option trading from various sources. They often start by relying on tip providers, then turn to news channels, and gradually attempt to learn trading from the so-called "YouTube University." Unfortunately, during this learning phase, many of them end up losing their entire capital and then seek out inexpensive courses in an attempt to gain knowledge.

They learn about indicators and price action, and think that *"ab aya hai unth pahad ke neeche"* (they've finally discovered the key to success). They start trading again after completing courses, even taking loans to fund their trades. However, they soon realize that price action works inconsistently, and candlestick patterns and chart patterns fail to deliver consistent results.

Now, the main crux of the matter is that sometimes price action may work according to their studies, but the option they bought doesn't increase in value. Can you relate to this? To be very honest, I was also in the same boat as you guys at some point.

I had received training from India's top coaches, renowned traders with a registered authority.

However, I did not achieve the desired results, I was on the verge of quitting trading when, fortunately, I came across my mentor from Dubai, who revealed the real secret knowledge about the stock market. I have written about him in the Author's Note.

The concepts I was taught were not easy to digest as they contradicted my previous knowledge. I had always heard that price action and various indicators were the only way to drive. But when I learned about the psychological aspect of trading, I couldn't convince myself.

Gradually, I gained trust in these studies, and when I started applying them, I got tremendous results. This study is called "THE MASS STUDY."

It is all about the true concept and the psychological way of trading.. My mentor told me, "GUNJAN, think like a businessman & plan your trades accordingly." This simple line changed my perspective because it holds deep meaning.

In any business, we need to convince our customers to get the desired price. Keep the word "CONVINCED" in mind. Now, think about the following 4 questions:

- Who is your customer in the stock market ?
- How can you convince them with proof?
- Who is truly treating this as a Business ?
- Are you treating this as a business ?

If you find the answers to these questions, the picture will change. Let me provide you with these answers so that your mind can start thinking from the other side of the table.

- **ANSWER 1**

Your customer in the stock market is your opponent.

- **ANSWER 2**

They can only be convinced by what they have been taught till now. Think about yourself as a retail trader. What would convince you? Is it chart patterns like double tops or bottoms, head & shoulder or flag patterns? Or would you be convinced when you hear it from someone whom you consider an authority, such as news channel editors or you consider YouTubers? I am not trying to prove anyone wrong here. I just want you to ask yourself: is that really the case?

- **ANSWER 3**

You are not treating this as a business because if it is a business for you, you would be making money or you start learning from someone who approaches it as a business, someone who thinks outside the box. If you are not doing so, that clearly means that you are not serious about this business. Even a small business owner also treats his business as a business by giving time, analyzing, and understanding about it, and if he feels that his business is not giving him results, he immediately finds someone who can help him learn about his mistakes. Now ask yourself, are you treating this as a business?

- **ANSWER 4**

Big players with a lot of cash treat this as a business. They have all the knowledge of the data and don't play blindly because business is not gambling; it can only be run on facts & figures. However, these biggies use tactics to make you believe that chart patterns are occurring or that a particular asset is acting according to the news. Do you know why? Because you are the customer for these guys.

Now, in a nutshell, you have to think out of the box. *Jo sabko dikhta hai vo nhi hoga, jo hoga vo dekhna mushkil hota hai, ke har koi nahi karta! What meets the eye may not come to pass, and what unfolds can be elusive to perceive. The ordinary seek simplicity, yearning for effortless experiences, where everything effortlessly falls into place.*

~Gunjan Arora

Before moving on to the next chapter, I want you guys to highlight the important points from this lesson and write them down so that you have a better understanding.

Chapter 10

GLOBAL MARKET

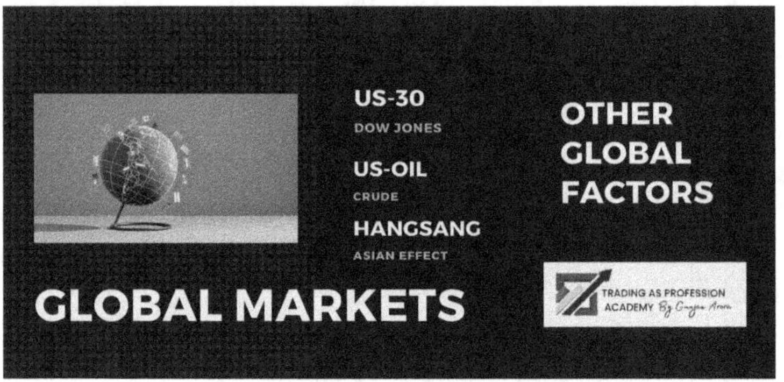

Now, this chapter is equally important as all the previous ones. I have the liberty to skip this lesson, but I am here to help you achieve success, which is within all of you. and Believe me, your success is just a step away now.

You can become a successful full-time trader by using the teachings I have shared so far. Honestly, there are many more things that should be kept in mind, as learning about the stock market is a long journey and you have to stay committed till the End.

The global market plays an important role in your execution. Why? This is because the Indian market has a large number of international players trading in our market, and their mindset, current situation, and currency fluctuations due to any kind of current affair will affect our market.

The biggest global market is the US market, and there are three major tradable indices:

1. S&P 500

2. Dow Jones

3. NASDAQ

You have to keep an eye on these indices for getting an overall idea of the sentiment. If the global market is bearish and our market is showing a bullish sentiment, most of the time the Indian market will not sustain its bullish trend. It is because the trend in the global market is very important for our market to align with.

Other global market to keep focus on are:

1. Hang Seng (major index in the Asian Market)

2. NIKKEI Index 225 (Japan)

3. UK 100 (UK market)

These Markets also play an important role in setting up the trend. So now we are about to conclude, and the last chapter is on execution of trades with all the information I have shared so far.

I have many more things to share with you, but I don't want to overload the content in a single book.

Chapter 11

EXECUTION OF A TRADE

The Final Process

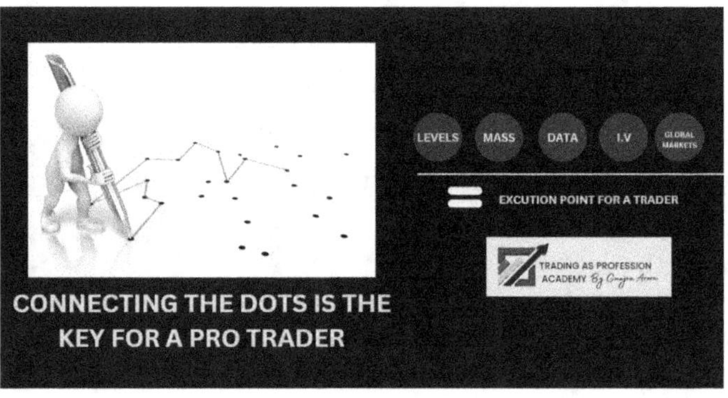

If you are someone who is directly trying to jump to this chapter so that you can get to the climax of the story, I suggest you go back and start from the first chapter.

I have shared the knowledge with you guys in a sequential way, as studying in a sequential manner is the perfect concept through which you will be able to absorb this content in your subconscious.

Honestly speaking, the content I am sharing with you is uncommon and not available on YouTube and it's not available commonly. My mind is still struggling while writing, as it keeps reminding me that my content is getting leaked. But my heart is saying that there are a lot of traders in India who are struggling, hoping that one day they will become full-time traders. They need your help. And my heart continues to win at the beginning of each chapter.

So once again, from the bottom of my heart, I am going to tell you about my framework of execution, which I have created and have been teaching in my academy for the past 4 years. More than 3500 TAP graduates are using this framework and making money daily.

I have a lot of case studies with me that have created magic for their families. I am sharing a few with you so that you can also use this framework for your trading career with blind faith.

"My Framework is Called as "MRSD=E"

Here is a case study of Sh. Kumar Mohan TR, who shares his experience with me and the MRSD-E framework.

The MRSD-E framework has everything required to earn money from option trading, and Gunjan Sir is the only magician who can teach this magic. I am proud to say that I am one of the oldest students of the TAP family and now a profitable trader too. Making money from option buying was never so easy.

~Kumar Mohan Tr
62 Years, Entrepreneur

Here is another case study of Swati Marda.

If I could have found your academy earlier, I would be a crorepati by now and an executing trader without fear. The market is working exactly as you have taught.

~Swati Marda
42, Advocate & Homemaker. Karnataka

The most sincere and heartfelt "THANK YOU" to Gunjan sir, who has provided us with support, guidance, and precious life lessons in trading. Your students, like me, will always keep you in their hearts. When it comes to teaching, no one can compete with you. You are the best teacher and mentor.

~Ram Avtar
Electrical & Engineering IIT Roorkee
Review Published On google

Such a hardworking academy, I have never seen before. All of the team members take care of us like family members. The experience I have gained here was beyond my expectations. I feel incredibly happy and grateful to TAP.

~Mandeep Singh
-42, M, Delhi
Review Published on Google

I have tried many stock market jugglers, but the aura of this man - Gunjan Arora, is amazing. His confidence is unmatched. The team is so great that you may try to find an escape route from doing homework, but they won't let you. They will make sure that you learn for sure. I never believed that such a sincere team operates in India, especially in the stock market. The teachings are not restricted to trading alone but also instill good values in life. THANK YOU for everything.

~Tania Gangully
Data Analytics, Hyderabad.
Review Published on Google

I have 100s of more case studies for whom I have created results, and many more on their way to becoming our next case studies. I have shared these case studies with you to show that if they can do it, then why not you?

In, MRSD-E
"M" stand for - MASS

This is a very extensive piece of content. It delves into the concepts of time correction in financial markets and the psychology of a trader. "MASS" is a concept that is intertwined with the nature of a human being who is also a trader and reading about price on charts from the other side of the table. It is such a vast topic that, I am considering writing a separate book solely dedicated to "MASS"

"R" stands for RBM

This is also Related to MASS only. RBM is all about time values in the financial markets and without using RBM, no trade can be a profitable trade. It's a guarantee.

"S" stands for S-series

This is a series on strategy creation that can assist you in developing your own strategy for any condition of the market. I always emphasize that a mere strategy will not suffice; a trader who possesses the ability to create a strategy for every situation is the one who can emerge victorious in the Game.

This is also a subordinate to "MASS"

By using S-series, one can create his own strategy for any kind of market situation.

"D" stands for DATA

Data is one of the most underrated, untapped, and often overlooked secrets of the F&O Trading. It's amusing to think that one can enter into options trading without having knowledge of the current and previous positions of the big players in the market as a whole. It is like driving a car at full speed on a highway with only knowledge of riding a two-wheeler. Anything can happen, God saves you.

"E" stands for Execution Part

We are now going to discuss this in detail. I am planning to write two more books as a continuation of this book so that you can derive the maximum value from my knowledge. Stay in touch with us to get updates. Stay in touch with us to get updates, you can Scan the QR code given at the end of the book and send your enquiry.

Now, with the knowledge I have shared so far, you can execute trades in options by connecting the dots. What dots? How to connect them? Don't worry, I am here to help you.

The 1st and foremost thing you have to do is to learn level-based trading. Level-based trading, along with the point of interest (POI), is the best ever gift I can give you. One special aspect to consider is that I am not talking about support or resistance based trading. For level-based trading, I have created a special video exclusively for the readers of this book. Scan the QR code below to access that video. After watching that video, return to read the next plan of action for execution. Make sure to take notes to enhance your understanding.

The 2nd action point for execution is the data reading. When I mention data reading, you might wonder where to find it and how to interpret it. Don't worry, I will provide you with detailed guidance. Let us divide this into three parts, which have been covered in previous chapters. However, here I will teach you how to connect all of them to take a trade effectively.

Part A: To read the data of an option buyer, you need to analyze the open interest of both call & put options. when the open interest on one side is increasing along with the price, it indicates a long buildup. Remember this information, as we need to consider a few more factors before making our decision. A long buildup on either side, accompanied by significant and intense numbers in both open interest & price, suggests the presence of option buyer on that particular side.

Part B: Data of an option seller, along with the data of an option buyer, it is essential to check the direction of the option seller. The option seller community is very powerful, and a careful examination of the data of an option seller is necessary to make informed trading decisions. When you observe a constant rise in the open interest and fall in price of that particular Options premium, it denotes the presence of of option seller's. If the numbers in OI are intense, it signifies that sellers are dominating on that particular side.

For example, if you observe a constant rise in the open interest of PUT options and at the same time, the price of those PUT options is moving lower, it indicates that option sellers are strategically positioning themselves to drive the market on the upside.

Now, keep this information in mind and cross-reference it with the data of option buyers exhibiting long build-up. If both the option sellers' data and option buyers' data align on the same side, it serves as a strong indication regarding the direction the market is likely to move in.

Part C : Now, it's time to analyze the data of future contracts. In both the previous parts, Part A and Part B, I have provided examples using index futures such as Nifty, Bank Nifty, or Finnifty. We need to examine the data of the respective future contract. If the price of futures is increasing and the open interest (OI) is also rising, it indicates a long build-up category. When the data of option buyer/option seller and the future contract align on the bullish side, it presents an opportunity to plan for a bullish trade.

Now, let's move on to the 3rd action plan, which is checking "implied volatility (IV)". After analyzing the data and planning for a bullish trade, it's important to consider the implied volatility. Let's take an example of buying a call option, it can be used for put option vice versa. If the IV is higher on the call side compared to the put side, it indicates that option buyers are entering the call side while put buyers are exiting their positions. This situation provides you a clue for the optimal entry point for bullish trade.

If by any chance, the implied volatility (IV) is not higher on the call side but higher on the put side, and the market is not moving lower, and all the data points are indicating bullishness, except for the higher IV on the put side, it suggests that the higher IV is fabricated. In this situation, there is a possibility of a false breakout in the market. As an option buyer, it may not be favorable to enter into a call option or put option. Instead, you consider being an option seller here by selling a put option.

Special Note Here: You may feel a sense of discomfort or difficulty in understanding this chapter, and I can relate to that because I had a similar experience. However, it is important to emphasize that you have no other option if you want to trade in options. I encourage you to read this chapter repeatedly until you gain a better understanding. Remember one new thing

"UNCOMFORT IS NEW SEXY"

"MY MENTOR"

4th ACTION Point is to check GLOBAL Sentiments.

If you are planning to execute a bullish trade while the global sentiment, as discussed in previous chapter, is bearish, I strongly advise against allocating your entire capital to this trade. Instead, consider allocating only 25% of your quantity in such circumstances. It's important to be cautious and consider the overall market conditions before committing a significant portion of your funds. If the global markets are moving in the opposite direction, most probably the IV factor will also be on the opposite side. In such cases, IV will not allow you to trade as an option buyer, making it challenging to execute profitable trades.

Keep in mind that if the US & Asian markets are not aligned in our favor, it will be very difficult to make money that day.

Now the main point:

After analyzing all this data, including IV and global sentiment, the next step is to execute trade after a confirmed break at predetermined levels discussed in the first part of this chapter.

You should have watched the video of levels-based trading. These levels serve as points of execution, indicating where you should enter and exit trades by connecting all the relevant dots. The information provided in this chapter is crucial for executing profitable trades and considering trading as a career. Up until now, you may have been making the mistake of losing money repeatedly. However, from this point forward, it's time to start making money. Let's consolidate all the information into a single chapter and review it.

Chapter 12

MORAL OF THE STORY IN A SINGLE PAGE

In this chapter, let's revise all the knowledge on a single page.

- I have emphasized the importance of checking data in Futures & Options.

- Chapter 2 provides detailed information on open interest.

- I debunked the myth of why option chains may not work for you during live market trading.

- I shared in-depth knowledge about the data of option buyers

- I explained the significance of the data of option sellers, including theta, delta, and vega.

- The data of the Future is equally important for making execution decisions.

- I provided a comprehensive calculation of open interest and how to analyze it.

- Implied Volatility is a key factor in option trading.

- I have discussed the Pyschology behind interpretation of the data and it's very crucial part and very necessary to understand for an option trader.

- The impact of global markets on our local Markets.

- The crucial aspect is the execution part and how to plan your trades effectively.

The Most Important Part Is The Execution phase, Where I Guide You On How To Plan Your Execution For A Trade.

All of this information is based on the best of my knowledge, and I can assure you that with a few months of practice, you will become a successful option buyer. You have the capacity and knowledge to do it yourself. I have shared this valuable content, which has been helping numerous people in our academy.

Here are some more case studies.

Just read this, what Manoj Upadhya has to say about this:

Learning from you has been a truly amazing experience which I cannot express in words. I am deeply grateful to have had the opportunity to learn from the best mentor in the world. Your teaching style is unique, and each lesson is incredibly important, directly impacting the subconscious mind. No doubt, after learning from you, one can make trading as his profession.

~Manoj Upadhay
Entrepreneur, MPK steel pvt. ltd. Jaipur
Published on Google

Read what Uttam Bangar has to say:

"Trading as a profession" is like a family. It not only develops skills but also enhances understanding of human psychology. He is not only knowledgeable and experienced but also friendly and supportive. He always made me feel comfortable and motivated.

He also provided valuable feedback and guided me in making important decisions. "TAP" has been a life-changing experience for me - I am thankful that I got selected for the academy.

~Uttam Bangar
IT Professional. Pune
Published on Google

Why have I shared the case studies with You?

I understand that some of you may feel a bit uncomfortable learning this, but I can assure you that it is not difficult, it "Needs Practice."

After practicing this skill, no one can stop you, "If These People Can Do It, Why Not You?" *sab ko mushkhi lagta hai* starting *mein,* (Many people initially have doubts), but after sometime, they are successfully making money from trading.

Now, before concluding this book, I want to ask you something. Let's come to the conclusion.

Chapter 13

CONCLUSION

It's Very Important *'Sab Yahi Chupa Hai'*

First of all, I want you to think by closing your eyes that,

Did You Get the Value & Knowledge?

If your answer is "YES," then don't give up. It's time for you to rise up and start practicing this skill. Here, you have two choices. You can either do it yourself alone, as I have shared a good part of my knowledge with you, and I appreciated that.

Or

You can do it with us as well, *hamare saath milkar kare*! You can have me by your side. You can apply for admission in our academy. We don't offer direct admissions or engage in selling courses. Our academy follows a deep academic culture, where we focus on the growth of each and every student. We have a Gurukul System in place, where group captains guide you throughout your journey. You will be assigned homework, and they will provide suggestions and support.

We are the only academy in India that teaches Data Reading Skills along with the Time Correction Concept on charts by using the (MRSD=E) Framework. If you are interested in admission, you can attend our 2- Day Workshop.

"The Trading Income Blueprint for women."

~Recommended for Beginners

Or

"The Option Income Blueprint
For pro TRADERS."

~Recommended for Traders with basic knowledge

In this 2- Day workshop, I will cover the topic of Data Reading and discuss all the content that I have taught you in this book through a live online Zoom Session.

You can scan or go to the Link below to attend the 2- day program. There is a small cost of 199/- associated with this workshop, and if you feel that you did not receive the value you expected, I offer a no-questions-asked money-back guarantee where I will refund your 199/-.

During these 2- day, only you will have the opportunity to apply for admission in our academy. We offer a 4-week Implantation Program where we provide guidance and support to ensure your success. Please note that without attending the 2-day workshop, you will not be eligible to apply for the Implantation Program.

P.S.: If you have already attended our 2- day workshop, please scan the QR code provided below to express your interest in the upcoming batch of the Implantation Program.

I hope I have added value in your life. Now, I want to give you some gifts. Let's move on to the next chapter to receive those Gifts.

Chapter 14

SPECIALLY CRAFTED FOR YOU

I want to Thank you for coming into my life and allowing me to fulfill my life's mission of teaching the Indian Community about the correct method of trading.

Thank You!

Thank You!

Thank You!

First Gift

I have been a student of Psychology for a long time, which has enabled me to think from the other side of the table.

I have created a special program for Mindset & Psychology, and I want to give that program to you. I have invested a significant amount of money (in lakhs) in learning about human Psychology, but I have made a pledge that I will never charge money to teach mindset & Psychology. So, here is the gift for you. Scan the QR code or click the link to access it.

Second Gift

As this book is not enough to provide you with the basic knowledge of price, candles, charts, and more, I have another gift for you. This gift is worth 4999/-.

"The Secret of Pro-Traders"

This is a basic course offered by our academy, and it's also available on our website for 4999/-. However, I want to give this gift to you for Free.

With this course, you don't need to learn the basics from any other YouTube videos or paid courses. I am known for giving gifts, so I decided to offer these two gifts to you to add even more value to your life.

There are a few more gifts for you.

1. Our VIP WhatsApp community

2. Our Premium Telegram channel.

With this, I want to conclude writing this book with full gratitude. Towards You.

SEE YOU IN THE ACADEMY!

~Gunjan Arora

TESTIMONIALS

(All these testimonials are published on Google review as well.)

"Wonderful experience, I learned 90% of my trading material from TAP journey.

Now, I can accurately assess whether my trades are going wrong or right during trading hours.

It's a genuine academy for learning trading. Our master, Mr. Gunjan Ji, is a person who is always full of energy and excitement, be it day or midnight.

God showed me the path to join this academy, so I am thankful to God."

~Virender Siwach
Bhiwani, Haryana

"Learning from you is really a very amazing experience which I can't express in words and from the bottom of my heart, I am very much thankful to God that I meet you and got an opportunity to learn from the best mentor in this world, you are really out of this world personality and your way of teaching is both simple and informative, directly hits our subconscious mind, your each and every story is very amazing, which makes it easy to learn trading or I can say even a novice can learn from you. As the name of your academy suggests, "Trading As Profession" No Doubt After Learning From You One Can Trade As Professional."

I want to continue with you in your next batch, and will pray to Krishna that you will take me in your next batch. I have surrender myself to you and want you to be my sarthi in this learning journey and in this new trading business venture.

I wish all the great success to dear Gunjan sir, our academy, and all its mentorship students, and all fellow students who are with us during this great journey of learning how to trade as a professional."

Regards

~Manoj Upadhyay
Mpk Steel Pvt Ltd, Jaipur

"Trading at Professional academy is really the last & final destination of a trading journey.

You cannot find any comparison of this academy in India, where you can achieve real success with utmost care for your trading journey."

~Pawan Kumar Dahiya
Ahemdabad, Gujarat

"Trading as Profession is like a family. It develops not only trading skills but also focuses on human psychology.

What to say about Gunjan Arora Sir, he is not only knowledgeable and experienced, but also friendly and supportive. He always made me feel comfortable and motivated in class. He taught me not only Trading skills but also personal development skills like human psychology. He also gave me valuable feedback and guided me for my improvements in trading.

The curriculum at the academy is well-designed and comprehensive. It covers all the necessary skills and topics that I needed to succeed in trading as a career.

TAP has been a life-changing experience for me, I am so grateful to the academy and Gunjan Sir for giving me this opportunity. I would highly recommend it to anyone who wants to learn trading skills in a professional and friendly environment."

~Uttam Bangar
Working professional, Pune

"A fantastic academy and a super fantabulous MENTOR.... So much concern for his students and such close interpersonal relationships....TRULY GOD SEND...Capacity Building at its best."

~Ashfaque Ahemed Lashkar
Tax consultant, Guwahati

"Excellent unbelievable experience, Gunjan Sir is outstanding, his knowledge, way of teaching and humbleness is amazing. He is a very nice person, I haven't seen such a genuine person. I don't have words to explain the class and Gunjan Sir, I want to continue this experience. All the best Gunjan Sir, God bless you."

~Rajkumar Vyahware

"Trading as a profession is very unique and standalone compared to others so called course sellers. Gunjan sir's way of teaching is unique. He taught us with real-life examples and showed you how our life is not different from trading. I love his caring nature for each and every student who is associated with him. He has an abundance of very very deep knowledge, if you follow his each and every word then you will be a successful trader in life."

~Ujjwal Kumar
Dombivli, Thane

"First of all, a five star rating is not enough to describe my experience with Trading As Profession.. This is not like professional classes who just want to sell their courses. TAP is a family of thousands of students who are learning each and every aspect of trading under our mentor Gunjan Sir... TAP not only teaches you about trading but it makes each student perfect and helps to evolve in every aspect of life.. Newcomers won't understand the importance of this Trading As Profession but those who have spent four-five years in the market and made huge losses will definitely understand it. So from the experience of older ones, the newcomers should also learn and join the TAP to start their success journey ASAP. *Hath pakadne chalna sikha hoga lekin yaha hat pakadne* trading *sikhate hai* sir.. With all due report love you Gunjan Sir."

~SAMRAT B
Ratnagiri

"Trading As Profession is the best academy of our country, they provide in-depth and actual knowledge of share market and its principal and nature.

I am proud to be a learner of this academy. Gunjan Arora Sir as the best super duper mentor. He is not only mentor but also like as a father."

~Rohit Mane

Pune, Maharashtra

"Trading as a profession has given life to many people who are lost in the world of stock market training, it is not just a training course, it is a Mentor/Guru who guides you and holds your hand always and always there whenever you need him. Thank you, Gunjan Sir, for being our Mentor. We are glad and blessed to have a person like you shaping our trading career."

~Mahesh

"Trading As Profession (TAP) ..I have joined this academy in AUG 2022 and I'm still a part of this beautiful family and will always be a part of this family! TAP is not only making me a successful profitable trader but also a good human being !! Gunjan Sir is the best mentor, best coach, best human being I have met so far, he is everything to me, his teaching is phenomenal. I can bet no one can teach the stock market better than Gunjan Sir !! To whoever reading my feedback I recommend you to join our academy (TAP) and learn the market from Gunjan Sir.....I repeat no one can teach you about the market like he does!"

~Saurabh kumbhalwar

UPSC aspirants, Gondia, Maharashtra

"Best place to learn and understand the psychology of trading. This study has in-depth knowledge in both Technical Charts and Data. Great combination.

Main focus of the whole team is the transformation of students into professional traders. For this, they put great emphasis on practice and revisions for best results.

Right place for right learning.

Best wishes to all."

~Gurusharan Bharaj
Entrepreneur, Pathankot, Punjab

"Guruji - There is a lot to learn from your coaching. Some of the concepts like MASS, DIG, CKT, TO and other Data analysis tools are new for me. Your free flowing coaching style is unique. Haven't seen such an energetic, committed and passionate mentor in my life. Your personal concern about the people 's development and financial improvement is remarkable."

"Tusi Great Ho Sirji. Please Continue The Same Spirit."

Regards

~Rajeev Agnihotri
Ex country head, MNC Delhi

"TAP is the place, where all your search for a real guru, who will guides you into right track make you a self-dependent TRADER, WILL END."

~Arindom Sanyal
Entrepreneur, Banglore

"Hello Everyone,

These lines only help those who want to be a Successful Businessman in the Stock Market.

Trading As Profession Academy is the best place to learn and grow, not only as a successful trader but also as an incredible human being. After joining the academy, I feel this is the family which I have been searching for a long time. Where I can learn, grow, earned and nurtured with skills and values by our Guru and Mentor Mr. Gunjan Arora. He is very approachable and excellent at coaching and mentoring. I received a Hand Holding experience of learning in this family.

Thank you Gunjan Sir, Thankyou, Kumar Sir, for giving me this opportunity."

Thank You God.

~Pritam Chaudhary
Entrepreneur, Rewari

"I have no words to explain. My life totally changed after joining TAP. Stock market is not what we see on YouTube. Stock market is a very different business. If you want to go dip in the stock market swimming pool then join tp. Sir's teaching style and Sir's interaction with students is very different from others. Just join in 99rs bootcamp. It's 99k value and selective people will get a chance to join only those who want to be hard core traders. Now, I am a part of the academy and the academy has become my family now. After following Gunjan Sir, I find myself more confident in life. I am 39 I have learned driving because of Gujjan Sir. I have thrown my fear out of my mind and became a more productive person in every angle. Now-a-days, I am closing all my trades in green only and this bcz of Gujjan Sir only. If you really want to be a hard core trader or pro in the stock market then join TAP.. Thanks again to Gujjan Sir and our academy members. Love you Sir from the bottom of my heart."

~Sikander Pathan
Entrepreneur, Mumbai

"Dear sir,

You are awesome! What you have taught us is very precious and out of the world knowledge. Your way of teaching is very cheerful.Your voice is very energetic. I really find myself very lucky to be a part of this trading journey. Your course really added super value in my learning and built a trading skill of option buyers. I am really thankful to you from the bottom of my heart. What you have given to me till now is precious compared to what I paid in the form of money. Keep continuing this Nobel work to make people financially independent. I really appreciate your genuine efforts towards training us in option trading, especially option buying. I hope I will start trading with conviction to earn daily profit following the trading rules and risk management taught by you. Your lectures on psychology and mindset were very much encouraging and educational towards building the trading mindset and patience while in trading. I am very fortunate to be a part of trading training with you. You are really an awesome teacher and nice human being. I found myself lucky, for selecting me for your mentorship course, and for giving me the opportunity to train under your guidance and providing your mentorship to grow myself in trading business and helping me to achieve my financial goal. Thank you with folded hands."

~Nishikant Dongre
Working professional, Kolkata

"If you want to become a trader this is the only course you will need. The knowledge and insights Mr. Gunjan Arora has is unique. You won't find this level of expertise in regular courses and on youtube.

His way of teaching is also very simple that every type of person can understand.

Just one thing is required that you unlearn everything you have learned or think you know about trading before joining this course.

There is also a very supportive community of past students; this is just like an academy. You can see him trade live. This is not some influencer who failed at trading who found they can make more money teaching the same things he read in books that made him fail.

Gunjan Arora is a trader with more than a decade of experience. He has reached such a level where he can trade so easily only after reaching this Zenith he has decided to teach a few people what he knows.

That is the mark of a true teacher or you can say Guru. First, you excel in your field and reach the highest potential and then you teach others and share the knowledge you have gained.

So, I strongly recommend Trading As a Profession academy, if you really want to trade full time or part time."

~Jairaj Sanand
Entrepreneur, Surat

"Truly a life changing and amazing experience of learning very effective 100% rule based trading with psychology and many more life lessons during 2 Hour Boot camp and 9 Days Masterclass. Trading As Profession is highly recommended as the need to look for any other course or mentor thereafter, will not arise after joining this. I feel blessed that I have joined and gained immense skill and correct mindset for being a successful trader. I urge all the aspiring traders to take the right decision to join Gunjan Arora Sir, without having a second thought and feel the change within yourself. Totally, extraordinary content packed with examples of real life successful traders. Thank you Sir, for giving this opportunity to be a part of you for your advanced courses."

Warm regards

~Jeewesh
Working professional, Mumbai

NEXT STEP

For any kind of support, we are here to assist you. Whether you have inquiries, concerns, or need assistance, please feel free to reach out to us. Connect with our dedicated team via email or phone to receive prompt and reliable assistance.

📞 +91 9372538978

✉ Care@tradingasprofession.com

NOTES:

NOTES: